D1456974

Mosaics

P. B. Hetherington

Mosaics

The Colour Library of Art
Paul Hamlyn·London

Acknowledgments

The works of art in this volume are reproduced by kind permission of the following galleries and museums: Antiquarium, Carthage [Rijksmuseum van Oudheden Exhibition at the Palais des Beaux Arts, Brussels, 1964] (Plate 20); British Museum, London (Plates 48, 49); Committee for the Excavation of Antioch and its Vicinity, Princeton University, Princeton, N.J. (Frontispiece): Corinium Museum, Cirencester (Plates 17, 18); Dumbarton Oaks Collections, Washington D.C. (Plate 46); Galleria dell'Accademia, Venice (Plate 42); Galleria Nazionale del Bargello, Florence (Plate 44); Musée Municipal, Lambese (Plates 12, 13); Musée National du Bardo Tunisia [Rijksmuseum van Oudheden Exhibition at the Palais des Beaux Arts, Brussels, 1964] (Plates 11, 14, 15, 19); Musei Capitolini, Rome (Plate 3); Musei, Monumenti e Gallerie Pontificie, Vatican City (Plate 8, Figure 3); Museo Nazionale, Naples (Plates 2, 4, 5, 6, 7, 10, Figure 2); Museo Nazionale, Rome (Plate 9); Museo dell'Opera del Duomo, Florence (Plate 47); Museum of S. Sofia, Istanbul (Plates 33, 35, 36); Staatliche Museen, Berlin-Dahlem (Plate 45); Verulamium Museum, St Albans, Herts. (Plate 16).

The photographs were supplied by the following: Agence Rapho, Paris (Plate 29); Alinari, Florence (Figures 2, 3, 4, 7); Paul Bijtebier, Brussels (Plates 11, 14, 15, 19, 20); Editions d'Art Albert Skira (Plate 1); Fotografia Ferruzzi, Venice (Plate 43); Ara Güler, Istanbul (Plate 33, Figures 5, 6); Michael Holford, London (Plates 9, 16, 17, 18, 23, 24, 50, 51); Denis Hughes-Gilbey, London (Plates 30, 31, 32); Mansell/Alinari, London (Figure 8); Josephine Powell, Rome (Plates 37, 38); Oscar Savio, Rome (Plate 3); Scala, Florence (Plates 2, 4, 5, 6, 7, 10, 21, 22, 25, 26, 27, 28, 34, 35, 36, 39, 40, 41, 42, 44, 47); Toni Schneiders, Photo Researchers, London (Plate 45); Raymond V. Schoder, S. J., Chicago, Ill. (Plates 12, 13).

Published by Paul Hamlyn Limited
Drury House · Russell Street · London WC2
© Paul Hamlyn Ltd 1967
Printed in Italy by Officine Grafiche Arnoldo Mondadori, Verona

Contents

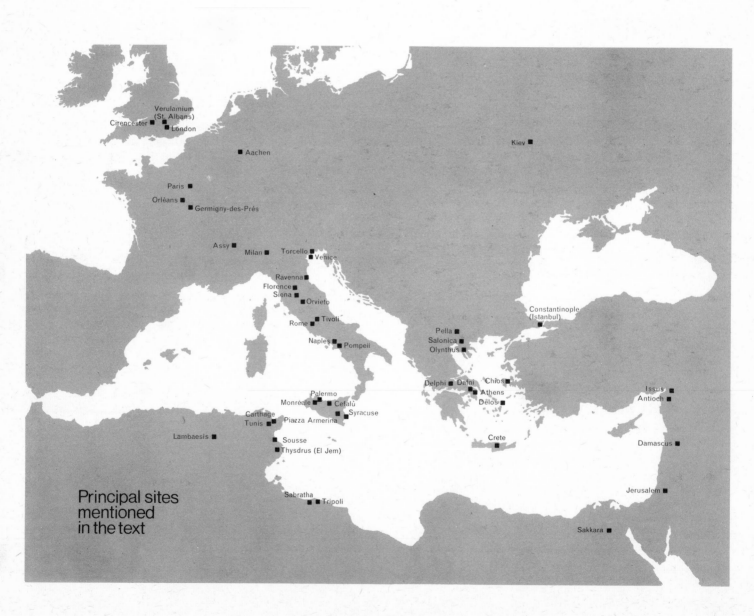

Verulamium
(St. Albans)
Cirencester ■
■ London

■ Aachen

Paris ■

Orléans ■
■ Germigny-des-Prés

Assy ■
■ Milan
Torcello ■
■ Venice

Ravenna ■
Florence ■
Siena ■
■ Orvieto
Rome ■ ■ Tivoli
Naples ■ ■ Pompeii

Palermo ■
Monréale ■ ■ Cefalù
Carthage ■ ■ Syracuse
Tunis ■ Piazza Armerina
Lambaesis ■
Sousse ■
Thysdrus (El Jem) ■

Kiev ■

Constantinople
(Istanbul) ■

Pella ■
Salonica ■
Olynthus ■

Delphi ■ ■ Dafni ■ Chios
■ Athens
■ Délos

Issus ■
Antioch ■

Crete ■

Damascus ■

Jerusalem ■

Sabratha ■ ■ Tripoli

Sakkara ■

Principal sites
mentioned
in the text

Introduction

The aim of this book is to provide the reader with an introduction to the main phases in the development of the art of working in mosaic, and the main usages to which the medium has been put. The most constant and persistent use of mosaic has been as an embellishment to architectural surfaces, and we shall follow its development in this field from the primitive two-tone designs of the earliest Greek mosaic pavements, direct and simple in their approach, through to the densely tapestried compositions of the richly pictorial mosaics which were laid like carpets on the floors of Roman and Pompeian houses. We shall see the tentative beginnings of Early Christian artists, striving for a new style with which to portray their new religion, emerge into the hieratic austerity of the Byzantine mosaic schemes where vaults and cupolas hold their images, as if embalmed, in a field of glinting, shadowy gold. We shall see how the new artistic principles of the Renaissance in Italy were incompatible with this direct treatment of the wall surface, and how it was really only in the gilded splendour of St Mark's, Venice, that the mosaicist's craft flourished down to the eighteenth century enjoying, as it were, a hot-house existence; and finally how it was the archaising trends of the later nineteenth century that brought about a revival of the medium, from which has developed a modern recognition of its potentialities.

The word 'mosaic' derives from the Greek word for the Muses, from which we can conclude that the technique of mosaic was associated with the highest forms of artistic expression. A mosaic is built up by the application of small pieces of roughly uniform shape, size and thickness to a field that can be either flat or curved; the word used for these pieces is *tesserae* or *tessellae* – again of Greek derivation, and it means 'four-sided', and is first used by Pliny when writing of the 'cubes' used in the making of pavements.

These *tesserae* are usually of an inorganic material such as marble, glass or shell. Any substance of an organic nature, such as wood, and objects inlaid with it, is therefore excluded from this study, as also are examples of *opus sectile*, in which comparatively large shaped plaques of marble or stone are let into a recessed surface.

The technique of mosaics is capable of wider usage and greater flexibility than any other decorative medium, and it is this which no doubt accounts for its very long history. Mosaics have been used to cover enormous areas of buildings, decorating both interior and exterior surfaces, but also can be reduced in scale to such an extent that they can form the design in a brooch or a ring. Between these two extremes there is still a wide variety of ways in which it has been applied; they range from the decoration of ritual masks from South America to copies of famous Greek paintings with which mosaicists decorated the floors of Pompeian houses.

Mosaic used with architecture

The art of mosaic has been most often used in association with architecture and it is in this field that it has perhaps attained its highest form of expression. As its use became better understood, so the inherent possibilities it had for the decoration of architecture became clearer, until in its most perfect form the mosaics and the building they embellish became fused into one homogeneous whole.

Mosaic, as such, is not found in the art of the ancient civilisations of the Near East. In Egypt the closest to it is in some of the rooms of the Great Pyramid of Zoser at Sakkara, where blue tiles are used to simulate wall-cover-verings and door rolls, but this appears to have been a solution to a particular problem in a decorative scheme, and does not represent a widespread type of mosaic technique. During the fourth millennium BC a form of decoration arose in Mesopotamia which approximates to later mosaic technique; an example survives in the palace of Warka in Chaldaea. Small cones of hardened clay, dyed with various colours, were pushed into the mud walls of buildings before they were dried, leaving the round bases of the cones to decorate the surface.

It was in fact left to the Greeks, in the humbler sphere of domestic floor-surfacing, to originate all later architectural mosaic decoration. The earliest remains that have so far come to light are in the form of pebble-mosaics that ornament the floors of buildings at several sites on the mainland of Greece – at Athens, Delphi, Pella, Olympia and Olynthus. In this rather simple but effective medium, chiefly black and white pebbles were used in both figurative and abstract designs, the black being used for the background and the white for the figures and pattern areas; sometimes dark red, green, grey and purple pebbles were also included, as in *The Lion Hunt* at Pella (plate 1). Examples of this early form

of mosaic from Olynthus are a useful starting-point, as they are known to have been produced before 348 BC when the town was destroyed by an earthquake, the earliest dating from about 400 BC. Some of the designs used are quite ambitious, such as a representation of Bellerophon killing the Chimaera, and it is possible that a scene like this may have been taken from a vase-painting, where the standard of artistic tradition was at this time higher. An alternative theory, which has quite a lot to recommend it, is that the whole field of these early designs represents the perpetuation in durable form of a tradition of carpet design. Textile fragments with designs similar to some of the Olynthus pavements have been found in South Russia, and this kind of merchandise could easily have found its way to Greece through the busy port of Corinth.

It was during the Hellenistic period that these comparatively simple beginnings can be seen to have developed into the form that mosaic has kept to modern times. With the introduction of regularly shaped *tesserae* of roughly uniform size a smoother finish was possible and the opportunities for a higher aesthetic content were increased. It is not known exactly when these flat, more regular *tesserae* were introduced, as our knowledge of the development of mosaic during the two centuries subsequent to the finds at Olynthus is uncertain; yet we do know, from literary sources, that the medium had advanced sufficiently in both prestige and technique for King Hieron of Syracuse (270-216 BC) to have some of the flooring in a ship that he had built decorated with scenes from the Iliad in mosaic of a variety of colours. These literary references are supported by the fact that large Roman ceremonial barges raised from the bed of Lake Nemi in central Italy actually had remains of mosaic panels in the deck.

It appears therefore, that even by this early stage in its development, mosaic had become subservient to painting.

It held this lowly status among the creative arts right through the classical era, so that the masterpieces of the Greek painters were still being faithfully copied by the mosaicists in Italy in the second and third centuries AD – more than four hundred years after their creation. The results of their work (for example plates 2, 5 and 6) are therefore more often technical *tours-de-force* in the translation of a painting into mosaic, than creative works of art in their own right. Nevertheless, they are of great interest since they are the closest reflections we have of the style and subject-matter of the Greek painters, and in some cases enable us to check the descriptions of their works by authors such as Pliny.

From archaeological evidence it would appear that the Romans applied mosaic much more to floors than to walls or ceilings. There are just one or two isolated exceptions, such as the Palace of Diocletian at Spalato (Split) where glass cubes were found loose on the floor in positions which suggested that they had fallen from the ceiling, that indicate that mosaic was used in this way. Nevertheless the general deduction holds good and even in huge decorative schemes like that at Piazza Armerina in Sicily or Hadrian's Villa at Tivoli, there is very little evidence that mosaics were used on any surface apart from the floors. Impressions left in the cement lining of wall-niches at Hadrian's Villa, as well as several decorative fountain niches remaining at Pompeii show that mosaic was, however, used to decorate wall features to a limited extent. The siting of mosaics in these earlier Roman buildings is more important to our subject than may be clear at first sight, for as we shall see, the earliest Christian mosaics of the fourth century and later are in fact to be found solely on ceilings and walls, and virtually never on floors. There are however literary references which throw some light on the problem.

Flavius Vopiscus, a Roman historian writing about AD 300, mentioned in his description of a wealthy citizen that 'it is claimed that he has clad his house in squares of glass set in bitumen and other preparations'. The passage is of great interest not only because it shows that the man in question had mosaics on the walls of his house at least, but also because it clearly reveals that there was no recognised technique for securing the *tesserae* to anything but the simplest surfaces – namely floors. It would indeed be surprising if any mosaics had survived still *in situ* on walls or ceilings after being set in such an unstable medium as bitumen.

At all events, it appears that we have to assume that the art of mosaic was relegated almost exclusively to floor surfacing; the weight of archaeological evidence supports this view, and the literary evidence quoted above implies at least that wall mosaics were the exception rather than the rule.

What are the implications of this? Firstly, there is the psychological disadvantage to which any artist is put, who knows that his work will receive heavy wear and even damage in the normal course of its use. This factor alone makes an example of such great richness and delicacy as the *Alexander and Darius at the Battle of Issus* mosaic (plate 2 and figure 2), an amazing phenomenon. Secondly, there is the fact that while a design is on the floor it can only be seen 'face to face' from a certain fixed distance – the approximate height of a man. As soon as the spectator moves away foreshortening distorts the image. This would encourage the repetition (at least as far as figurative designs were concerned) of a selection of well-known compositions that could be quite easily recognised, and which were provided to a large extent by the masterpieces of the Greek painters of antiquity, such as Aristides of Thebes, Sosos of Pergamum and Nicomachos of Thebes.

This slavish reproduction of earlier works must in turn have appealed more to the artisan than to the creative artist, and so the situation arose where the practice of a certain art form was confined to a large extent to a class of technicians who were not equipped to realise its full potentialities as a medium. They were simply concerned with the execution of a kind of permanent picture.

A further explanation might be offered for the humble position occupied by the mosaic in the normal domestic decorative scheme. We have long known and admired the subtlety and sophistication of the illusionistic painted frescoes that decorated the walls of Pompeian houses. It may have been realised that neither the surface quality of mosaic, nor the limited number of colours available, would have been suitable for illusionistic purposes. The emphasis given to the wall surface by the use of mosaic would have been the opposite of what was intended; the space of the room would have seemed more enclosed, rather than opened out into the illusionistic vistas which were desired.

The earliest extant examples we have of the kind of mosaic that was referred to as being let into the deck of King Hieron's ship in the third century BC, are those on the island of Delos, of which one of the finest depicts Dionysus riding on a panther. It is of the late second century BC, and already considerable elaboration has been attained. There also appears to be a definite attempt to create something that is in itself precious, set into a large surrounding frame. Not only are the *tesserae* of the animal and figure smaller than the dark background area, but various kinds of marble are used and even semi-precious stones such as onyx and agate, besides coloured glass paste. The cement between the *tesserae* is tinted to match them and to conceal the joins as far as possible.

This mosaic is also an early example of the use of an *emblema*. This is simply an area of mosaic – usually quite small – that was made up separately from the rest of the floor and mounted on a tile or slate. These *emblemata* were produced by specialist workshops at a number of centres, which supplied mosaicists throughout the Graeco-Roman world. That the Greek mosaicists working in Greece and Italy did not appear to be worried by the effect of these small compositions of densely-set, small *tesserae* surrounded by much larger areas of plain or patterned mosaic on a larger scale, implies a surprisingly under-developed architectonic sense.

The Roman mosaic floors of the late first century BC begin to do away with these *emblemata*, and by the first and second centuries AD the 'all-over' pattern is predominant. The small mosaic panel of *Sea Creatures* (plate 7), *Actors* (plate 4) and a *Still Life* scene (plate 6) are all from the period before the 'all-over' pattern had become accepted, and were set like cabinet-pieces in a large surrounding frame.

Pompeii, the rich, pleasure-loving city south of Naples, which was engulfed in an eruption of Vesuvius in AD 79, had an unparalleled collection of mosaic floors of this type; many have been taken from their original surroundings and are now on the walls of the Museo Nazionale in Naples. It is easier to study and admire the technique of the works when they are displayed in this way but a very considerable effort of imagination is needed to visualise them in their original setting. The largest, such as the *Alexander and Darius* mosaic would have had the appearance and quality of a rich carpet, but one has to imagine the smaller panels, such as those illustrated in plates 3 to 7, as set in a large overall pattern made up from larger, and perhaps more roughly laid, *tesserae*. These small areas of finer *tesserae* must have appeared as interruptions in the surface of the mosaic and must have constituted awkward breaks in the homogeneity of the design.

This practice had died out early in the beginning of the Christian era, and all-over designs with *tesserae* of more or less uniform size were introduced. From this period onwards we find increasing numbers of Romanised works of art, including many mosaic floors, produced in the provinces of

2 Alexander and Darius at the Battle of Issus

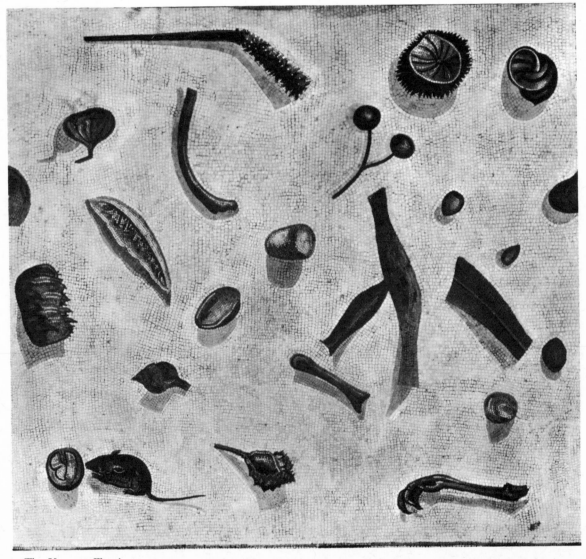

3 'The Unswept Floor'

the empire. This naturally gave rise to so-called 'provincial' mosaic workshops in areas like North Africa, Gaul and Britain, but this 'provincialism' is apparent in the execution rather than the design; the design and supervision of the work must have been the responsibility of a trained craftsman, though labour may have been recruited locally. One example of this development in Roman mosaic is the mosaic of *Personifications of the Seasons* from Cirencester (plate 18). The overall design is close to many second-century floor mosaics all over the Roman Empire, but the unevenness of execution suggests the participation of a local assistant. The design, however, and that of the *Scallop-shell* from Verulamium (plate 16), shows an appreciation of the problems of filling certain areas of floor-space which is not apparent in many of the Pompeian designs. The late third century, in such schemes as the huge ensemble at Piazza Armerina, Sicily, produced the Roman mosaicists' most satisfactory solutions to the problems posed by the limitations in both shape and siting of the floor surface.

There is, of course, a very large group of classical mosaics of abstract design with no figural representations at all; indeed surviving examples of this more limited, abstract use of the medium probably exceed the number of representational mosaics from the classical world. These patterns might be built up of repeating units, as in the impressive example which survives from the floor of the Baths of Caracalla in Rome, or they could take the form of a single overall pattern fitted to an entire floor area, such as the illusionistic mosaic from Antioch (frontispiece).

What, then, did the mosaicists of the classical era achieve? In the first place they established the medium as the normal method of surfacing the floors of public or private buildings that were of any importance. Their early subservience to painting meant that they were at a disadvantage when it came to creative design. It may have been the link with a naturalistic style of painting that prevented mosaic from developing any further at this time; the classical mosaicist was, as we shall see, faced with the problem which confronted the artists of the early Renaissance: the creation of an illusion of pictorial space with a medium that draws attention to its surface. Certainly it would seem that the art had gone as far as it could and was ready for a new aesthetic point of departure.

By about AD 300 a fresh outlook and a new impetus had become necessary if the art of mosaic was not to stagnate and wither for lack of direction and creative purpose. It was in the early years of the fourth century that just such a reviving force was provided.

EARLY CHRISTIAN AND BYZANTINE PERIOD

The greatest turning-point in the history of the Christian religion, and possibly in the history of the western world, occurred in the year AD 313, when the Roman emperor Constantine the Great (272-337, emperor from 306), officially recognised Christianity. From its inception the Christian church had suffered intermittent bouts of persecution, one of the most concerted being that carried out under Diocletian in 305; but from 313 the Christians were free to worship as they pleased and, of great importance for our purpose, to decorate their places of worship as they wanted.

There were undoubtedly already buildings in use as churches before 313, as we are told that many churches were destroyed in Diocletian's persecution of 305, but it is probable that any artistic decoration they may have had was of a fairly humble sort, running parallel in this respect with the art of the catacombs. Although many of the earlier emperors had been tolerant of Christianity, they had not actively supported it, and the religion had not gained any wide following in the upper levels of Roman society. The result was that the earliest Christian art, prior to the fourth century, tends to reflect the taste of the lower social strata. A small third century Christian vault mosaic has in fact recently been found in excavations beneath St Peter's, Rome, but in general mosaic was very seldom employed, both because of its pagan associations as well as its cost.

As we have just seen, the mosaicists of antiquity displayed considerable limitations in the practice of their craft; it was in the overcoming of just these two limitations that the mosaic art of the Christian era was to achieve its greatest works, and set a standard of architectural and decorative unity that has seldom, if ever, been surpassed.

In the first churches to be built under official imperial patronage mosaic decoration was not a matter of course. Constantine wrote to Archbishop Makarios of Jerusalem concerning the building of the Church of the Holy Sepulchre 'Moreover I should like to hear your opinion as to whether the apse of the basilica should be coffered, or decorated in some other manner'. It was therefore still a matter of choice: coffering, or some other decoration such as mosaic. However, the latter was very soon established as the medium that was most acceptable from every point of view for church decoration, and particularly for the apse.

Many of the fourth-century Roman mosaics are now lost. Probably the first large-scale Christian mosaic was that in the apse of the basilica of St John Lateran, but others such as those in the basilicas of St Peter's and St Paul's were soon to set a precedent that was repeated in countless variations all over western Europe. This concentration of mosaic, the richest known decorative medium, on the curved surface of the apse clearly had a symbolic significance for the early church; this part of building may perhaps have been associated with the vault of heaven.

The earliest Christian mosaics of any size to survive are those in the vaults of the church of Sta Costanza in Rome (plate 21 and figure 4). The mosaics of this rotunda, which originally covered the inside of the dome as well as the ring-vault, still echo in style the impressionistic treatment of Hellenistic wall-paintings. The subject-matter, although now Christian in intention, is basically pagan in origin; the grape-harvest subject, probably adapted from a floor-mosaic, has become a reference to Christ's metaphor of the vine and the branches. Other panels in the ambulatory show a mystifying assemblage of late antique decorative motifs with no apparent unity of content.

The fifth-century panels in the nave of the basilica of Sta Maria Maggiore, in Rome, illustrate the development of this early Christian mosaic style; one of the surviving panels of the original forty-four is shown in plate 22. The *tesserae* are used in an obviously impressionistic manner to suggest rather than to describe the forms of the figures, and the debt that the artist owes to the tradition of Roman imperial art is very evident. The priest Melchisedek is shown offering bread and wine to an Abraham (see note to plate 22) whose pose is identical to that of the equestrian monument of the Emperor Marcus Aurelius in the Campidoglio on the Capitoline Hill in Rome, and many other details of these scenes from the lives of Abraham, Jacob, Moses and Joshua reflect the imperial origins of early Christian iconography. Here also we can see for the first time the extensive use of gold *tesserae* which in some of the scenes indeed completely negates any sense of atmosphere; in other scenes groups of figures move in skilfully suggested space under a sky that is delicately dappled with clouds.

The use of mosaic in these two conflicting ways – one to suggest space, and the other to negate it – in a single series of scenes marks the mosaics of Sta Maria Maggiore as a monument of transition. The distortions and exaggerations of the Abraham and Melchisedek composition are an indication of the efforts that fifth-century Christian artists were making as they groped their way towards a new pictorial language and technique. The gradual dissolution of the late antique pictorial style can be followed in a sequence of monuments in Rome, such as the apse mosaic of St Cosmas and St Damian (plate 23), from the early sixth century, the chancel arch mosaic of St Lorenzo-fuori-le-mura (plate 24), from the late sixth century, and the apse mosaic of Sant'Agnese, dating from the early seventh century (plate 25). While one describes in negative terms the loss of realism and negation of space in examples like the Abraham and Melchisedek scene, one can see in Sant'Agnese what this means in positive terms. The three figures present themselves to the spectator motionless and impressive; there is no conflict between volume and space or between movement and repose. The figures are transcendental, weightless images.

Meanwhile, there had been developments in other parts of Italy. The unsatisfactory position and status of Rome may have been partly responsible for the second momentous decision of Constantine; in AD 330 he dedicated Byzantium, then a small Greek town on the Bosphorus, as the official, new capital of the Roman Empire. This action, which transferred the real seat of power to the eastern Mediterranean, had a number of momentous after-effects; one of these was the decision by a later emperor, Theodosius (374-395), to divide the Empire between his sons, leaving Arcadius ruler in the east and Honorius ruler in the west. In 402 Honorius moved his capital from Milan to Ravenna, a town on the east coast of Italy. Our interest in Ravenna centres upon the rich series of mosaics still adorning its churches for these provide us with a bridge between early Christian art and Byzantine art.

The earliest monumental mosaics that are left there are in a small, cruciform building now called the Mausoleum of Galla Placidia. The sister of Honorius, Galla Placidia was closely connected with the ascendancy of Ravenna, and the

4 Interior of Sta Costanza, Rome

mosaics that cover the upper parts of the Mausoleum named after her, date from her death in 450. Blue is the predominant colour, and the small dome over the crossing is decorated with gold stars against a dark blue background – an unmistakeable re-creation of the heavens at night. Other parts of the vaults have formalized star designs set in a pattern over the blue. There are several subjects shown in other parts of the building; St Lawrence walks towards the gridiron on which he was martyred, doves are shown drinking at the water of life, and in the semicircular lunette over the door is a mosaic representation of Christ as the Good Shepherd (plate 26). All these mosaics are clearly designed to be in harmony with, and to complement, the architectural members of the building. So that whereas the mosaics of Sta Maria Maggiore have really very little relationship to the architecture of the church, in the Mausoleum of Galla Placidia there is a large degree of unity between the structure and its decoration. What is still lacking, however, is the internal unity of the mosaics themselves; in spite of many attempts it has simply not been possible to find a unified scheme for the varied subject-matter. Internal unity of this kind was to be achieved only in later works but meanwhile the idea of fusing mosaics and architecture into one interdependent structure was further developed and gave rise to some magnificent results.

Theodoric the Goth, who captured and reigned at Ravenna until his death in 526, commissioned a number of buildings, of which the chief surviving is the church now called Sant'Apollinare Nuovo; this title in fact dates only from the ninth century, when the saint's remains were transferred from the basilica at Classis, a few miles outside the town. The mosaic decoration is now confined to the nave, and consists of three principal bands; the lowest of these represents processions of martyrs, male down one side and female down the other, walking towards the altar; the middle band includes the windows, between which stand mosaic representations of prophets and patriarchs; the upper band contains thirteen scenes from Christ's life and miracles, and thirteen from the Passion. Without going into the theological problems involved, it will be seen (plates 27 and 28) that although the style of both the series is identical, the representation of Christ varies, being bearded only in the Passion scenes. The continuous processions of martyrs establish a feeling of unity between mosaics and architecture by emphasising the longitudinal element in the nave of the basilica, whereas the Passion scenes, reminiscent of the panels in Sta Maria Maggiore, could be regarded as a regressive element in so far as they tend to break this unity.

The mosaics of San Vitale, however, show not only a clear intention on the part of the mosaicists to decorate the architecture and emphasise its structural tensions, but also an awareness of the need for unity in the subject-matter. The well-known mosaic on either side of the apse, showing Justinian and Theodora presenting offerings, are of the first examples of true, imperial Byzantine art. They are not true portraits, but serve to legalise the Emperor's power, in the same way as did his images, erected in towns conquered by Byzantine forces; the image was believed to contain the sanctity and power of its prototype, so that although neither Justinian nor his Empress ever set foot in Ravenna, their authority was maintained there by these mosaics.

As we have seen, floor mosaics were rare in Christian churches (the Justinianic basilica at Sabratha in North Africa with its vine-pattern floor mosaic is an exception), the mosaicists' art being concentrated on the walls and cupolas. As the art of the Christian mosaic developed, it diverged from the classical tradition not only in the siting of the work, but also in the style and we can follow a gradual dematerialisation of the convincing, naturalistic forms of late antiquity; at Ravenna this reached a sufficiently hieratic,

5 Bolting Mule

6 Camel with Children

spiritual quality for us to say that truly Byzantine art had been born. Although we can surmise that the mosaics of Ravenna reflect developments in Constantinople, no churches survive there with sixth-century mosaics still in place.

There is, however, one set of mosaics that is of even greater interest, as it allows us to see what mosaicists did when working on secular projects. The floor of a court in the Royal Palace of the Byzantine emperors in Constantinople has been excavated in recent years, and it shows us a completely different world from the mosaics of San Vitale, with which it is probably roughly contemporary. In the first place it is a floor mosaic. One has to go back to Roman floor mosaics like those at Piazza Armerina to see a similar kind of treatment and mosaic style. The subjects depicted are small, isolated illustrations of animals, children, pastoral scenes, etc. The people and animals shown are often depicted in quite complex foreshortening, like the goat being milked, and the realism of the modelling is of a high order; groups are even shown in violent action, such as a man with a bolting mule (figure 5). Surely, nothing could be further in subject, sentiment and treatment from the hieratic poses of the figures in San Vitale. What we are looking at here is an example of a tradition of court art that must have survived into the sixth century in the court surrounding the 'King of the Romans', as the Byzantine emperor styled himself. It must have been a rather self-conscious attempt to maintain the spiritual link with the ancient Roman Empire of the West, but in its lack of unity of subject and its use of clearly second-hand classical motifs, there is the suggestion of a dying art, lingering on outside its original tradition.

During the eighth and early ninth centuries the art of the Byzantine mosaic was greatly affected by the official ban on the representation of Christ and the saints, which initiated that period in Byzantine history known as the age of iconoclasm. The ban was in force for almost one and a quarter centuries; not only were no images produced in Byzantium and any areas in close touch with it, but existing images were destroyed, defaced or covered up. The motives behind this policy were complex, and need not detain us here. This policy was inspired both by theological objections to idolatrous abuse of images, and political considerations; the full complexity of its motivation need not detain us but its effect on the practice of mosaic decoration was naturally very great and this we must look at. The craft did not die out, but it had to turn to different fields for its subject-matter, and particularly to buildings concerned with the faith of Islam, then a rising power which also forbade images in its places of worship.

With the final restoration of images in the mid-ninth century there evolved a kind of pictorial formula to which any religious image had to conform if it was to be a true aid to worship. Any image had to be a recognisable likeness, and names were written in to make identity quite certain. The representation was to act almost as a receptacle for the spirit of its prototype, and in order that the worshipper could then enter into communication with the saint, the image was always shown in strict frontality. Any figure shown in profile or back view was simply 'not present' to the beholder. What all this meant for the mosaicist's craft can best be seen in the eleventh century, when the most fully integrated and finely balanced mosaic schemes of the Byzantine era were created. Ninth and tenth century mosaics like those in the cupola of Hagia Sophia, Salonica and provincial eleventh century ones like those at Kiev in Russia may be looked on as experiments out of which the 'classic' schemes of the eleventh century were evolved. In these the arrangement of the mosaics is completely absorbed into the forms of Byzantine church architecture, and these in turn are dependent upon their decoration for their significance to be fully understood. Thus the building and its mosaics finally

7 The Annunciation, with Aaron and St Stephen

become fused into one homogeneous entity. There are only three examples of this 'ideal' mosaic scheme still in existence; one is in the church at Dafní, a few miles from Athens, another is in the Nea Moní on the island of Chios, and the third is in the church of Hosios Loukas, near Delphi, the most complete of the three. They differ in various respects and it is probable that the 'classic' system was always adapted and modified to suit local conditions.

The mosaic decoration of a Middle Byzantine church would ideally be divided into three 'zones', or areas, placed in a descending order of sanctity. The first zone, in the highest part of the church, would contain the most sacred images; the centre of the main cupola was reserved for Christ as Pantocrator — the 'All-powerful' (plate 30), while the conch of the apse was always used for representations of the Virgin (plate 31). The second zone is lower down in the structure of the church, and is concerned with the scenes from Christ's life which are depicted in the squinches which support the main cupola; the chief events from Christ's life and the major feasts of the Church are shown here, such as the Annunciation (figure 7), Nativity (plate 32), Presentation, Baptism, Crucifixion and *Anastasis* (Resurrection). The lowest zone, which occupies the vaults and upper walls, is concerned solely with images of saints from the Church's calendar (figure 7). The saints depicted are again subject to local variations, so that there is no invariable rule as to which can or cannot be shown; indeed variations in the size of churches alone makes a regular number impossible: Hosios Loukas had originally about one hundred and fifty, while Dafní and the Nea Moní had less than forty.

It will be seen from this brief description that the mosaic scheme was, as it were, 'suspended' from the central cupola with its roundel of the Pantocrator, and it is this feature of Byzantine church architecture that separates it from the western, Gothic conception of a church, where the whole feeling is one of 'soaring' weightlessness. The sensation to the spectator of a Byzantine church, with its central cupola supported by squinches, and lower down by the vaults, is one of a 'hanging' architecture, with only the apse to suggest a direction within the building.

From all this we can conclude that the architect and the foreman of the team of mosaicists (if, indeed, such single, specialised occupations existed) worked in very close partnership; it has been suggested that the architect and the director of the mosaic 'workshop' were one and the same man. If they were not, it is obvious that the closest collaboration was essential when one considers some of the subtleties that are worked out in the relationship of the mosaics to their setting. Taking the *Annunciation* scene (figure 7), for example, one can see how the designer of the mosaic has made use of the concave shape of the squinch to get as near as possible to the illusion of the Angel actually talking across real space to the Virgin; he has produced what Demus calls a 'spatial icon'. Similarly, in the *Nativity* (plate 32) the angels are bowing before Christ in the most literal sense; the curve of the mosaic field emphasises this movement from whatever direction it is approached. It is also possible to see how the re-entrant quality of the mosaic area has been exploited to provide the illusion of the cave actually receding into the mountain where the event is taking place.

This complete integration of mosaic and architecture grew up with a specific architectural form – that of the Byzantine church with its Orthodox liturgy and ceremonial. During the twelfth century the Norman kings of Sicily saw the possibilities of mosaic as applied to a basically Gothic church architecture, and Byzantine mosaicists with varying amounts of help from local craftsmen decorated the un-Byzantine interiors of their basilical plan churches in the three towns of Cefalù, Palermo and Monreale.

Faced with the problem of applying a standard mosaic scheme to a church with a strong longitudinal axis and (in two cases) no cupola, these craftsmen developed a characteristically logical solution. The conch of the apse became the holiest and most important part of the church; the image of *Christ Pantocrator* was placed there (plate 34) and the rest of the decoration was subordinated to it. The walls of the nave were taken up largely with scenes from Genesis, and other cycles. The Cathedral of Monreale is the most complete example of this phase in the history of mosaic decoration, many thousands of square feet of the interior being encrusted with richly decorative scenes.

Besides Sicily, where the twelfth century witnessed this phase in the 'westernisation' of a specifically Byzantine art form, there was one other principal centre to which Greek craftsmen came to design and set mosaics, and where local workers learned their technique, namely Venice.

This city, built on the north Adriatic coast of Italy, had for centuries had close trade links with Constantinople; its chief glory, the church of St Mark's, was actually built as a copy of the Church of the Apostles in Constantinople, and so it was natural that when the Venetians came to embellish it they should choose a characteristically Byzantine medium – that of mosaic. The area involved was immense: five principal cupolas, the apse and all subsidiary vaulting, besides nine smaller cupolas in the narthex and baptistry, and many smaller areas such as niches over doorways on the façade and inside (plate 39 and figure 8). It is not surprising, therefore, that although work began in the late eleventh or early twelfth centuries and activity was sustained during the thirteenth and into the fourteenth, the completion of the scheme and the restoration and replacements of the mosaics was carried on almost continuously into the nineteenth century (plate 42 and 43).

A quite definite Veneto-Byzantine style was formed, which was an assimilation of Byzantine, Romanesque and local

8 Interior of St Mark's, Venice

Venetian elements, but the decorative scheme did not conform to any overall plan. The mosaics of the apse, main cupolas and narthex were among the first to be done and the work of the sixteenth, seventeenth and eighteenth centuries is often adjacent to that of four centuries earlier, producing a strange conflict of styles (figure 6); the great unifying factor is the glow and flicker of the millions of golden *tesserae* which cover every inch of the background. The general effect, indeed, offers the modern visitor the closest approximation to the sixth-century Church of the Apostles in Constantinople that he can hope for.

Meanwhile, in the late thirteenth century, there was a last flowering of mosaic in Constantinople itself which had fostered the art for so long. During the greater part of the century, from the sack of the city in 1204 by the fourth crusade until the collapse in 1261 of the Latin 'empire', Constantinople was the capital of a line of western usurpers, but after their expulsion a new wave of church decoration seems to have begun. The large Deesis in the South Gallery of Hagia Sophia (plates 35 and 36) was almost certainly a result of this movement. The softer modelling of Christ's face (which is quite close in feeling to that of the somewhat later work in Monreale) is contrasted with the superbly expressive St John, whose beard and clothing are depicted with an amazingly rich variety of coloured *tesserae*.

The culmination of this halcyon period in Byzantine art, when the Palaeologue dynasty ruled a diminishing empire, was the decoration of the Church of St Saviour in Chora, known more often by its Turkish name of the Kariye Camii. While a lot of the early fourteenth-century decoration is in fresco, an extensive series of mosaics occupies the outer and inner narthex, illustrating for the most part scenes from the life of the Virgin, as told in the apocryphal and canonical gospels (plates 37 and 38). The donor of the mosaics was Theodore Metochites, at the time Logothete, or Counsellor, in charge of the imperial treasury, who is portrayed over the doorway into the church from the inner narthex, offering a model of the church to Christ. It is interesting to see to what extent Byzantine court dress had become orientalised by this time; although the emperor persisted in calling himself King of the Romans, Greek had been the official language for centuries and oriental elements predominated in Court life and ceremonial. The mosaics depict a completely different aspect of traditional Christian subjects from what had been the traditional canon. Instead of the hieratic austerity of Hosios Loukas, we have here figures in movement, even in conversation, inhabiting space that is to some extent defined. The humanity that is apparent in such a subject as the *First Seven Steps of the Virgin* is something quite new in Byzantine art. It is an interesting reflection that Giotto had only just completed his frescoes in the Arena Chapel in Padua when these mosaics were executed.

RENAISSANCE AND LATER PERIODS

While these new developments were taking place in the East, the first stirrings of the Renaissance were being felt in Italy. One symptom of this new attitude was in the re-emergence of the artistic personality; towards the end of the thirteenth century for the first time since antiquity, artists began putting their names on works of mosaic, and the Roman artists such as Pietro Cavallini and Jacopo Torriti signed their names in inscriptions on mosaics in two Roman churches. The anonymous tradition of the Middle Ages had been broken. Artistically, this new outlook took longer to show itself in such a definite way. Nevertheless, if one looks at Cavallini's scene of the *Death of the Virgin* (plate 40) one can see definite attempts to model the forms solidly, indeed the artist is clearly embarrassed at trying to show figures in space with a medium which draws so much attention to its own decorative surface. The decorative band of pure pattern that runs along the top of the scene peters out when it meets the architecture of the background, suggesting that Cavallini was aware of the inconsistency.

Other artists of the early Renaissance used the medium of mosaic; Torriti worked at Sta Maria Maggiore, Rome, and even Giotto executed the famous Navicella in Old St Peter's in mosaic. But the fact remains that the artistic outlook of the Renaissance was not one in which the medium had any real place. The humanist Leone Battista Alberti, was one of the first to lay down the principles on which Renaissance artists based their painting. In his treatise *Della Pittura* he defines his attitude to painting as a 'window into space'. It is quite clear that the surface of the painting is intended to 'disappear' as far as is possible, linear perspective being one of the ways in which this effect was to be brought about. This emphasis on the construction of pictorial space, and the consequent dematerialisation of the picture surface, finally sealed the fate of mosaic as a major art form. Artists, particularly sculptors, continued to use it, but usually in a subordinate position such as a background to set off marble sculpture; Arnolfo di Cambio and Orcagna both used it in this way, and it may have been this kind of example that inspired Donatello's use of blue glass discs in the background and columns of his Singing Gallery. The family workshop of the Cosmati, however, continued a tradition of mosaic into the fourteenth century, decorating church furniture with abstract patterns of gold, red, black, grey and white mosaics. Floors, columns, pulpits, heavy marble candlesticks and bishops' thrones were all adorned with the characteristic Cosmati mosaic patterns. But this in itself implies a lower status; it had become what is now called an 'applied art'.

The practice of decorating architecture with pictorial

mosaics continued a tenuous existence outside Venice into the sixteenth century. In 1497 David Ghirlandaio executed an Annunciation in mosaic for the SS Annunziata in Florence, and when Raphael designed the Chigi Chapel in Sta Maria del Popolo in Rome, he actually designed cartoons for decorative panels under the dome, which were then carried out in mosaic by a Venetian, Luigi del Pozzo.

However, Venice was the stronghold of the tradition, and the workshops of St Mark's provided a constant training ground as well as eventual employment for a group of specialists. The mosaic of *St Mark in Ecstasy* (plate 41) is a good example of how they were employed. An established artist, in this case Titian, provided a design which was then interpreted by the mosaic technicians, in this case two of the Zuccato brothers. This example is also interesting because it so clearly illustrates the corruption of the medium through the attempts of artists to model a solid figure in a material that so clearly emphasises its surface quality. In addition to this, the gold background which originally held intimations of infinite space, is here rendered pointless by the puff of white cloud out of which comes the hand of God. What has happened? Ultimately, it is simply mis-use of a medium; but this kind of mis-use would scarcely have been possible before the fifteenth century, since it was only during that century that *tesserae* began to be produced in a sufficiently wide variety of colours to permit the subtlest, almost infinite, gradations of tone. To some extent, then, we may say, it was the skill of the manufacturers of the glass *tesserae* which led to the abuse of the true nature of the medium.

The zeal with which the Venetians restored or replaced the mosaics of St Mark's produced even more extreme examples of this kind; the lunette mosaic *St Mark* (plate 43) over the second entrance from the north end of the façade, is almost nearer to fresco-painting in its effect than to mosaic. It was perhaps reaction to works such as this, combined with the renewed emphasis on the picture surface, largely characteristic of painting since Cézanne, that produced the revival of mosaic as a serious artistic medium in the twentieth century.

Mosaic applied to portable objects

It may be that mosaic was first generally used in the field of applied decoration rather than in conjunction with architecture. A stone box, excavated at the palace of Knossos by Sir Arthur Evans, contained fragments of rock-crystal, amethyst, beryl, lapis lazuli and gold, which appear to have been intended for the ornamentation of furniture; indeed mosaic may have been used for domestic objects of this kind at an even earlier date, during the Middle Kingdom of ancient Egypt, though the dividing-line between mosaic and inlay is very blurred at this remote period. We can be certain, however, from literary references, that mosaic was used for this purpose in the classical Roman period.

It will be remembered that up to the first century BC floor mosaics often had a central *emblema* produced off the site in a specialist workshop. It appears that it was also possible to have these framed and hung as paintings, as Suetonius describes how Caesar used to carry these *emblemata* about with him on his campaigns. This may have been a widespread practice, as some of the *emblemata* that have survived are known to be copies of lost works by famous Greek painters of antiquity; a good example is the famous *Doves Drinking at a Bowl* (plate 3). To hang such a mosaic panel on a wall, rather than have it set in a floor, would merely be to restore it to its rightful position. Some of the houses in Pompeii contained original panel paintings by the Greek masters, and these paintings were treated with the utmost care, being kept in a box or in a shuttered recess in a wall. But to possess a 'reproduction' of such a work in a durable form like mosaic would be a natural way of enjoying a famous work of art, without the anxiety and expense of owning the priceless and fragile original. This specific use of portable mosaics as the ancient equivalent of the modern gallery reproduction probably continued up to the end of the first century BC, when production of these *emblemata* seems to have ceased. Unfortunately, none of the surviving classical mosaic panels of unknown provenance can certainly be said to have been used in this way; in most cases like that of the *Lion Bound by Cupids*, in the British Museum, it is clear from their condition that they have been extracted from a floor.

It was not until the Byzantine mosaic icons of the late eleventh to mid-fourteenth centuries that portable mosaics of this kind were once more produced. One must, of course, distinguish between these specially-produced portable mosaics, and fragments that have become detached from a wall in the course of time; the only real test for this is a technical one. True portable mosaic icons always have the *tesserae* set in wax or resin, and are mounted on a panel or board. Although all these Byzantine icon mosaics are so late, it is not impossible that they represent a remote survival of a classical art form absorbed over the centuries into the tradition of Christian art.

The rarity of these mosaic icons (only about thirty survive) and their precious, jewel-like quality combined with other stylistic and iconographic peculiarities makes it virtually certain that they were manufactured in Constantinople itself. Indeed, there is good reason to believe that they were solely for the use of the circle of the Court and in the services in Hagia Sophia. Some of the larger examples, such as that of *Christ the Merciful* (plate 45) in Berlin, have *tesserae* on a scale that is not very different from monumental mosaics. It is usually thought that this implies an earlier stage in the development of the form, since later examples (plates 46 and 47) have an astonishingly fine technique, with minute glass *tesserae* which give a brilliant and glowing effect to the surface.

The pieces of mosaic jewellery, produced in Italy from the mid-eighteenth century, are on an even smaller scale. These are the first known examples of this type of jewellery, but it would be surprising if there had not been attempts of this kind in earlier periods which have not survived. At all events, a selection in plates 50 and 51 shows the scope and skill of the Italian craftsmen who had the monopoly of this particular form of mosaic; the smallest pieces are no bigger than a fingernail. The subject-matter of some of them suggests that they were sold as souvenirs which could be subsequently mounted; that of a basket of flowers, set in lapis lazuli, was in fact probably mounted for use as a pendant. Mosaic could scarcely go further in the direction of polished, gem-like elegance than this.

Various forms of mosaic technique must also have been widespread in cultures outside the European sphere; and the Aztec works shown in plates 48 and 49 provide very striking illustrations of the rich effects achieved. Both the ritualistic character of these objects and the precious materials of the applied mosaic decoration, make them particularly apt examples of the art of the Aztec craftsmen. Obsidian, garnet, quartz, beryl, malachite, jadeite, marcasite, mother-of-pearl and above all turqouise were used to adorn the ceremonial shields, helmets, knives, and other articles of ritual. An especially characteristic use of this rich mosaic decoration was its application to ritual masks and to the skulls which played an important part in the rites of the ancestor cult.

It is interesting that once they had left their original environment, both these objects of Aztec ritual and the Byzantine mosaic icons appealed to the same kind of collector's taste, on account of their precious materials. The two largest collections of mosaic icons were those of Pope Paul II and Lorenzo de' Medici (Il Magnifico), and the latter, under Leo X or Clement VII eventually came to include the collection of Aztec ceremonial objects presented to Cortes by Montezuma II.

Notes on technique

Although methods of laying mosaics have varied to some extent through the centuries the basic needs of the medium have imposed on the artist a sequence of operations which has remained fairly standard.

First, the surface to which the mosaic is to be applied has to be roughened to provide a good hold for the first layer of cement. This is, of course, less essential for floor mosaics than for those on walls or ceilings, where the cement has to 'key in' to the surface more firmly in order not to fall away when dry. This first layer is pitted all over while it is still wet with the trowel-point or some other instrument to provide further purchase for the subsequent layer; as shown in plate 36, which illustrates a section of mosaic with this first cement bed exposed. At this point one, two or even three layers of finer plaster can be applied, the floor or wall surface being first thoroughly wetted and all precautions taken to ensure that each layer adheres firmly. This stage provides an intermediate bed which in turn then receives a final layer of plaster, approximately the thickness of the *tesserae* to be used; this is left smooth, and the design either drawn or traced onto it. The method of applying the design has varied considerably. Now, the most common method is to use a large area of paper to transfer a design, but this would not have been practicable before the fourteenth century, and traces of underpainting on the setting-bed have often been found, showing that the design was laid in with a free brush.

After the design had been applied the usual practice was for the plaster to be chipped all over, wetted, and the final setting-bed applied. This would be done in areas small enough to be covered before the plaster hardened. He would then press the *tesserae* into the plaster, normally working from the top of the mosaic field downwards so that previous work was not spoiled by falling plaster; any wet plaster left at the end of a day's work would be scraped off. From earliest times it was common practice to tint the plaster that pushed up between the *tesserae* so that the design would not be obscured by the criss-crossing white lines.

There are many unknown factors in the formation and working methods of the mosaic workshops of antiquity and of later periods, but an edict (vii. 6.) of Diocletian (died AD 313) gives us valuable and specific information since it enumerates the various jobs in a workshop and states the wage rates, thus revealing the comparative status of the workers. At the head of the organisation came the *pictor imaginarius* who was paid 175 *sesterces* a day. He was not only the artist who provided the design, but in all likelihood directed the whole operation and allotted the various jobs to the other men. Next came the *pictor parietarius*, the draughtsman who applied the design to the setting-bed; his wage of 75 *sesterces* implies that his job was fairly mechanical, requiring no originality and little special skill. Finally, there were the workmen who actually carried out the design: the *lapidarius structor* (stone mason), the *calcis coctor* (preparer of the plaster), and the *musearius* (the technician who actually set the mosaic *tesserae*); this comparatively unskilled labour was paid for at the rate of 50-60 *sesterces* per day.

Quite an early development in the craft of mosaic was the multiplication of the colours in which *tesserae* were available. The Delos mosaic of *Dionysus riding on a panther* (late second century BC) shows that about fifteen colours were used, made from marble and semi-precious stones, and, even at this date, coloured glass paste. The number of shades increased steadily, although they were not all necessarily used, as in the *Alexander* mosaic (see plate 2 and note). Gold *tesserae* were probably used as early as the fourth century; they were manufactured by encasing a fragment of gold leaf between a thick and a thin piece of glass which were then fused. By the fifth century about forty-five colours and shades, as well as gold, were available as can be seen from the mosaics of Sta Maria Maggiore.

It was eventually the skill of the Venetian glass workers at producing an infinite number of different shades of colours that contributed to the virtual abandonment of the medium of mosaic. Once it had become possible for the mosaicist actually to counterfeit the subtle gradations of colour effect found in fresco painting the point of his medium had been defeated. An interesting illustration of this impasse is provided by a lawsuit brought against the Zuccato workshop by the Venetian Senate in 1563. The Senate alleged that the Zuccati had been saving themselves the expense of providing and working the *tesserae* by producing faked mosaic effects in paint. The case was submitted to a panel of eminent artists consisting of Titian, Sansovino and Tintoretto, who, after inspecting the work found that there had in fact been an attempt to deceive the Senate.

If the increasing range of colours was one important element affecting the development of mosaic, another was the skilful way in which the Byzantine mosaicists learnt to exploit the actual siting of their works on wall surfaces. To take one example, the *tesserae* of the mosaic in the lunette over the door of the entrance vestibule in Hagia Sophia, Istanbul, are all set at an angle of 13° to the vertical; the result is that the individual facets do not appear distorted to the spectator as he stands below and looks up at the mosaic surface.

Cupola mosaics, where figures are shown standing round the base of the cupola, also reveal this consciousness of the spectator's view-point. They are often given elongated proportions, particularly of the lower parts of the body, so that when seen from below the figures would appear to be 'right'.

Notes on the illustrations

Frontispiece *Illusionistic Floor Mosaic.* From a house near Antioch. 2nd century AD.

Many patterns such as this were invented and exploited by the later Roman mosaicists; unlike many earlier designs, these would almost certainly have existed only in the medium of floor mosaic, and not have derived from some other art form. Nevertheless, the idea of a floor mosaic used in the way of a carpet has been maintained.

Figure 2 *Alexander and Darius at the Battle of Issus.* Museo Nazionale, Naples. Late 2nd century BC.

This large mosaic was discovered in the 'House of the Faun' in Pompeii in 1831. Although now displayed on a wall, it was originally a floor mosaic. Its present position can be justified by the fact that it has the exceptional interest of being a copy of a painting of the fourth century BC by a Greek artist, probably Philoxenos of Eretria, whose composition of this subject is described by Pliny (Nat. Hist. 35. 110.); claims to its authorship were also made for Aristides of Thebes and Helena of Alexandria. The neutral strip along the bottom implies that even the proportions of the original have been accurately reproduced, the shape of the room in which the mosaic was laid not quite conforming to that of the composition. (See also plate 2).

Figure 3 '*The Unswept Floor*'. Musei, Monumenti e Gallerie Pontificie, Vatican City, (Formerly Museo Laterano, Vatican City). 2nd century AD,

This fragment of Roman mosaic is a copy of another floor mosaic by Sosos of Pergamum the celebrated Greek artist of the second or third centuries BC. It was one of the most famous examples of *rhyparography*, or the painting of sordid or insignificant subjects, as opposed to *megalography*, the painting of subjects that were larger in importance as well as scale (see figure 2). Here the skill of the artist is almost solely concerned with the trompe l'oeil effect of the floor of a *triclinium* (dining-room) before the scraps left over from the banquet have been swept away.

Figure 4 *Interior of Sta Costanza.* Rome. 4th century AD.

The church of Sta Costanza was built 326-330 by Constantine the Great, and was used as a mausoleum for his daughter Constantina (died 354). The plan of the building is circular with an added portico, and the mosaic panels in the ring-vault over the ambulatory, which we see in this view, are therefore trapezoidal in shape, and curved to fit the architecture. The entire cupola was also covered with mosaics which have disappeared since the sixteenth century. There is every reason to date these and the existing mosaics as contemporary with the building and the panel mosaics are among the earliest ceiling mosaics to survive. (See plate 21.)

Figures 5 and 6 *Bolting Mule* and *Camel with Children.* Details of Floor of the Great Palace, Istanbul (Constantinople). Probably 6th century.

These scenes, with a number of others, are to be found in one floor mosaic which is still *in situ* on the site of the Great Palace of the Byzantine emperors to the south east of Hagia Sophia in Istanbul. This floor (originally round a large peristyle court, 70 yards square) is of the greatest interest as it is the only example discovered of a figural floor mosaic from a secular building of the Byzantine era. The subject matter includes mythological subjects, a number of hunting scenes and some bucolic subjects involving animals, children, etc. These are distributed over the whole floor area except for the border (a strip about a yard wide); there is no reference to a consistent view-point or a common ground. This floor shows that when Byzantine mosaicists were not portraying the mysteries of the Christian faith, they were still able to work in the realistic tradition of the late Roman artists. The two styles of depiction, religious and secular, were carried out concurrently.

For archaeological reasons the floor cannot be dated before AD 400. In the light of its obvious debt to late antique art the date was first thought to be about AD 410. Scholars have since dated the work later and later, and now a date in the reign of Justinian (527-565) or even Justin II (565-578) seems most probable. The area has still not been completely excavated, and major evidence may yet come to light.

Figure 7 *The Annunciation, with Aaron and St Stephen*. The Catholicon, Dafní, Attica, Greece, Late 11th century.
The monastic church at Dafní, a few miles from Athens, was rebuilt in the last quarter of the eleventh century, and its mosaics are contemporary with this rebuilding. This view clearly demonstrates the way in which the Byzantine mosaicists exploited the three-dimensional shape afforded by the squinch in order to increase the realism of the event portrayed (see page 21). It also shows how the saints and prophets were placed in the vaults and niches lower down, forming the third zone of decoration. (See also plate 30.)

Figure 8 *Interior of St Mark's, Venice*. 11th century, with mosaics of a later date.
First founded in 828, the present building was erected in 1063-1073 by the Doge Domenico Contarini as a chapel for the Doge's Palace; Venice had close connections with Constantinople, and this church with its five domes is one of the very few copies of the Church of the Apostles in Constantinople, now destroyed but used for centuries as the mausoleum of the Byzantine emperors.

This is a diagonal view over the crossing from the height of the gallery, towards the mosaics of the *Entry into Jerusalem* (plate 39) and *The Temptation* of Christ, with the seated figure of St John the Evangelist in the squinch, and mosaics of a later date on the inside of the eastern arch. (See also plate 39.)

THE PLATES

Plate 1 *The Lion Hunt*. Pebble mosaic. Pella, Macedonia. About 300 BC.
The ancient Greek city of Pella, a few miles from Salonika in northern Greece, was the capital of Alexander the Great's empire; it appears that this was one of the first centres in antiquity to develop the technique of pebble mosaic. Tiny, water-worn pebbles of three or four different basic colours were used, the outlines of the forms sometimes being strengthened by embedding strips of lead on edge in the setting bed. All the later achievements of the great Hellenistic artists are latent in this superb series of mosaics, of which plate 1 is an example.

Plate 2 *Alexander and Darius at the Battle of Issus*. Detail. Museo Nazionale, Naples. Late 2nd century BC.
The Battle depicted took place in 333 BC at Issus in Cilicia (see map); Alexander the Great defeated Darius, the Persian king, although the latter actually escaped. The artist chose the moment when the tide of the battle had just turned in Alexander's favour, and plate 2 shows the figure of Darius in his chariot as he flees from the youthful Alexander. The strange headgear of the Persian can be taken as a fairly accurate rendering of Eastern costume of the period.

The mosaic is of exceptional size, and approximately 1½ million *tesserae* were used in its construction. Although by the second century many more colours would have been available to the mosaicist, he has limited himself to four principal ones. This could be because Nicomachus, the master of Philoxenos, (see note to figure 2) was a noted four-colour painter, and the colours of the original have thus been faithfully preserved.

Plate 3 *Doves Drinking at a Bowl*. Musei Capitolini, Rome. Probably 1st century BC.
This mosaic *emblema* was found in one of the floors in Hadrian's Villa in 1737. Like plate 2 it is of particular interest as being a copy of a lost painting by the ancient Greek artist Sosos of Pergamum (see note to figure 3), that we know of from an admiring reference by Pliny. Although to some extent restored, the liveliness of the design and the fineness of the execution can easily be appreciated, each square inch of the surface containing over sixty *tesserae*.

Plate 4 *Actors in the Wings of a Theatre*. Museo Nazionale, Naples. 1st century BC.
This small panel, originally set in the floor of the 'House of the Tragic Poet' in Pompeii, must reflect the interests of the owner of the house. The mosaic shows actors preparing themselves for a performance and is interesting in that it shows figures in action in a mosaic that is unlikely to have been copied from a Greek painting. The early use of *genre* is also of interest, in that the actors are seen in preparation, formally, rather than in their parts on the stage.

Plate 5 *Street Musicians*. Museo Nazionale, Naples. Probably 1st century BC.
Originally set in the floor of the 'Villa of Cicero' in Pompeii. The inscription which reads: ΔΙΟΣΚΟΥΡΙΔΗΣ ΣΑΜΙΟΣ ΕΠΟΙΗΣΕ means 'made by Dioscourides of Samos'. There is uncertain, ty as to whether this refers to the mosaicist or to the painter of the original scene of which this is a copy. Together with a companion panel also at Naples, this is one of the very few known examples of a signed mosaic composition in antiquity. Another, poorer quality copy of

the same scene was found at Stabiae, so it would seem that the inscription refers to the painter of the original.

Plate 6 *Cat Catching a Bird and Still Life with Ducks*. Museo Nazionale, Naples, 1st century BC.
This panel was originally set in the floor of a room in the 'House of the Faun' in Pompeii. In its acute observation of the animal world it prefigures exactly the type of still-life painted by the Dutch seventeenth-century painters.

The separation of the two scenes by a narrow white line emphasises the fact that the ultimate intention is only to decorate the surface with brilliantly composed scenes, rather than to create an illusion of pictorial space.

Plate 7 *Sea Creatures*. Museo Nazionale, Naples. 1st century BC.
This panel was found set in the floor of the *triclinium*, or dining-room of a Pompeian house. At first sight one might be looking through the wall of an aquarium, but on the left there are some rocks from which a bird looks down; the basic qualities of the design are decorative although the observation and depiction of the individual species of fish are a *tour-de-force* of the mosaicist's skill.

Plate 8 *Pastoral Scene of a Herd of Goats and a Rustic Sanctuary*. Musei, Monumenti e Gallerie Pontificie, Vatican City. 2nd century AD.
This scene was part of a floor mosaic in Hadrian's Villa at Tivoli, not far from Rome. Its mood reflects the pastoral ideals expressed in such Latin poetry as Virgil's *Eclogues*; no particular event or person is depicted. This rustic atmosphere is subtly expressed by the softly atmospheric effects achieved by the mosaicist, whose fully Hellenistic 'impressionist' technique can still be appreciated, despite heavy restoration.

Plate 9 *Fisherman's Hut on the Nile*. Detail from the Barberini Mosaic. Museo Nazionale Archeologico Prenestino, Palestrina. lst century AD.

The celebrated but much restored Barberini Mosaic depicts an Egyptian scene during the flooding of the Nile. It is a unique work, giving a wealth of topographical detail very sensitively handled, and is of exceptional size, being surpassed in this respect by only a very few works of the scale of the *Alexander* mosaic (plate 2).

Plate 10 *Portrait of a Lady*. Museo Nazionale, Naples. lst century BC.

Originally set in the floor of the *cubiculum* of a house in Pompeii, this mosaic probably represents the *domina* or mistress of the house, whose memory was thus perpetuated. It is the only surviving example from antiquity of a portrait in mosaic, and reflects the same qualities of realism as some of the so-called Fayum portraits from Egypt carried out in wax encaustic medium.

Plate 11 *Ship at Quayside*. Floor-mosaic at the threshold of an underground tomb. Musée du Bardo, Tunisia. Mid 3rd century AD.

This floor mosaic with a representation of a ship in a harbour was excavated at Sousse in North Africa in 1890. From its style and quality it is clearly the product of provincial mosaicists; the rendering of the sea, particularly, by roughly parallel serrated strokes, although giving a fine effect of pattern has nothing of the atmospheric naturalism of the *Goats and Rustic Sanctuary* in the Vatican Museum. The very ambiguity of the placing and actions of the figures, and their disproportionate scale underline the provincialism of the work as well as its late date.

Plates 12 and 13 *Nereids Riding on Sea-monsters*. And Detail.

Lambese Musée Municipal, Algeria. 2nd century AD.

The Nereids were the daughters, traditionally fifty in number, of Doris and Nereus, the 'Old Man of the Sea'. This floor mosaic from a house in the Roman colony of Lambaesis in North Africa shows Nereids riding on the back of fantastic sea-monsters; the billowing veils arching over the figures are a hallmark of classical figure-compositions, which was copied right into the fourteenth century (plate 37). The mosaic is signed at the bottom in Greek characters: ΑΣΠΑΣΙΟΥ 'the work of Aspasius'; this demonstrates that even to this date Greek artists were the principal ones of the Roman Empire.

Plates 14 and 15 *Bacchic Procession. Detail of the Camel with Silenus on its Back*. Thysdrus (El Jem). Musée du Bardo, Tunisia. 2nd century AD.

This floor mosaic of a Bacchic Procession was excavated at the entrance to the *triclinium* of a house in El Jem, North Africa, in 1959. It shows the young god Bacchus riding on a lion, led by a Bacchante with a musical instrument like a tambourine and a satyr with pipes; behind are Silenus on a camel, another Bacchante and a panther. In the background are Bacchic symbols. The motif of the young god Bacchus riding on a lion is of Hellenistic origin, and is symbolic of the power of the god over Nature.

Plate 16 *Scallop-shell*. Verulamium Museum, St Albans, Hertfordshire. Probably 2nd century AD.

This scallop-shell mosaic is from the floor of the apse, or alcove, of a room in a house in the Roman city of Verulamium; the house was built about AD 130-150 and there is no reason to suppose that the mosaic is any later. It is a good example of the way second–and third-century mosaicists became more conscious of the shape of the floor for which they were designing.

Plates 17 and 18 *The Seasons* and *Autumn* (Detail). Floor Mosaic. Corinium Museum, Cirencester, Gloucestershire. 2nd century AD.

This floor mosaic, typical of much of such work in the Roman provinces, was designed to contain eight octagonal frames. Those at the four corners have allegorical figures of the four seasons, and the variations in the quality of the heads shows that an assistant, probably of local origin, must have been employed; that of Spring is noticeably cruder than those of Summer and Autumn. Summer is shown naked, while Autumn is clothed and decorated with grapes and vine-leaves, and holds a pruning-knife.

The theme of the four seasons recurs in Roman mosaic floors found at Bignor, in Sussex, and at Chedworth, Gloucestershire, indicating that it was to some extent a standard subject.

Plate 19 *Still Life with Flask and Beaker*. Musée du Bardo, Tunisia. Late 2nd century AD.

This floor-mosaic is part of an ensemble that decorated the floor of the *triclinium* of a house at El Jem, North Africa, excavated in 1903-4. The whole floor was originally divided into 21 fields by leaf-garlands, each one containing either an animal or a small still-life group. Still-life had been a common subject for fresco-painters up to the second century AD, but had not been used much by mosaicists. When compared with the *Still-life with a Cat* (plate 6) it can be seen that this is a less well-observed, more provincial work, besides being considerably later.

Plate 20 *Woman with a Halo and Sceptre*. Portrait bust. Antiquarium, Carthage, North Africa. Late 4th or early 5th century.

This panel was in the centre of the room of a late antique house excavated at Carthage in 1953. Its subject is uncertain, and one tends to associate the style of the depiction–the large eyes, frontal pose and even the halo–with sixth-century mosaics like that of Theodora in Ravenna. However, one is forced to suppose that this is a Christian figure from its halo, sceptre and the gesture of the right hand, and it is probably either some personification or an angel, which would have had special significance for the owner of the house.

Plate 21 *Vault Mosaic Panel*. Sta Costanza, Rome. 4th century See also figure 4.

The main inspiration for the decorative theme of this mosaic was probably a pagan Bacchic floor mosaic that was adapted to fit this particular area. It illustrates very clearly the debt that much of Early Christian art owes to late Antique art forms. The portrait bust framed by the decorative vine-scrolls may possibly be that of Constantina, for whom Constantine built the mausoleum.

Plate 22 *Abraham and Melchizedek*. Nave mosaic. Sta Maria Maggiore, Rome. Probably 5th century.

Sta Maria Maggiore was rebuilt under Pope Sixtus III (432-440). The mosaics that decorate the interior fall into two groups; those on the chancel arch, which contain only scenes of the Virgin and Christ; and separate mosaic panels down each side of the nave (there are 27 left out of the original 42), with scenes of the Old Testament figures of Abraham, Jacob, Moses and Joshua.

The scene of Abraham offering bread and wine to Melchizedek is taken from Genesis XIV, *18*, and is a good example of the inherent symbolism of the cycle. Abraham is shown as a conquering emperor on horseback, while Melchizedek, King of Salem, brings forth bread and wine. This is one of the classic scenes from the Old Testament that pre-figure the events of the New Testament – in this case the institution of the Eucharist; to emphasise this the elements are shown as greatly exaggerated–the wine in a great urn stands in the centre of the foreground, and the loaves of bread fill a basket directly above it. To make the point even clearer this is the nave scene that is nearest to the altar where the Eucharist would be celebrated.

Plate 23 *Christ and Pope Felix IV, with SS Cosmas, Paul, Peter, Damian and Theodore*. Apse mosaic. Church of SS Cosmas and Damian, Rome. 526-530.
This church, built in the Forum in the old temple of Maxentius, is the earliest example of the transformation of a temple into a church. The mosaic in the apse was created under Pope Felix IV (526-530), and though still retaining much of the massive, dynamic quality of late antique art, has just begun to show some of the qualities of dematerialisation that were to become more evident in the next two centuries. (It should be pointed out that the figure of the Pope was completely re-set in the seventeenth century).

This design for an apse mosaic was immensely influential in Rome, being repeated with variations right into the late thirteenth century. The twelve sheep approaching from left and right symbolise the twelve apostles, who converge towards the Lamb of God raised on a small mound in the centre, from which issue the four rivers of Paradise.

Plate 24 *Christ and Pope Pelagius II, with SS Lawrence, Peter, Paul, Stephen and Hyppolitus*. Chancel arch mosaic. Church of St Lorenzo-fuori-la-mura, Rome. 578-590.
Pope Pelagius II (578-590), who built the original basilica in honour of St Lawrence, is seen on the left of this group, holding a model of the church. Contemporary with the later mosaics of Ravenna, this arch mosaic is a perfect document of the transition that took place in Rome from the late antique style (see plate 23) to that of the fully schematic figures of the seventh century (see plate 25).

Plate 25 *St Agnese and Popes Symachus and Honorius*. Apse mosaic. St Agnese, Rome. 625-638.
The titular saint of the church, St Agnese, is shown standing between Pope Symachus (495-514) holding a bible, and Pope Honorius (625-638) who holds a model of the basilica.

An attempt was made to martyr St Agnese by burning her alive but the fire was extinguished miraculously. The symbolic flames are shown at her feet. She was in fact killed by a soldier, and the blade of the sword is shown in front of her feet. Her richly jewelled crown of martyrdom is seen above her, held by the hand of God.

This is one of the most extreme examples of the incorporeality attempted by Early Christian artists seeking a pictorial metaphor for the divine.

Plate 26 *The Good Shepherd*. Lunette mosaic. The Mausoleum of Galla Placidia, Ravenna. Mid 5th century.
The mausoleum of Galla Placidia may have been built as the oratory of an adjoining monastery; it is constructed on a Greek cross plan, and the view shown here is that of the lunette over the door in the north wall, with the barrel-vault adjoining it.

The Good Shepherd was a common Early Christian subject, and the beardless young Christ here depicted was clearly based on the classical type of Apollo or Orpheus. This mosaic probably represents our nearest clue to the mosaic style current in Constantinople in the fifth century.

Plates 27 and 28 *The Betrayal* and *Christ Dividing the Sheep from the Goats*. St Apollinare Nuovo, Ravenna. Early 6th century.
The church of St Apollinaire Nuovo in Ravenna was built by Theodoric, King of the Ostrogoths (493-526) as his cathedral. These scenes are taken from the top band of mosaic decoration in the nave, which consists of 13 episodes

from the life and miracles of Christ on the north wall, and 13 scenes from the Passion on the south side. The style of the figures shows a growing orientalising tendency, while the iconography is derived from the Early Christian art of the catacombs, or from the Roman imperial tradition.

The Betrayal of Christ is shown in stark, narrative form, the two groups confronting each other, with Judas leaning forward to kiss Christ while Peter grasps his sword to cut off Malchus' ear.

The depiction of *Christ Dividing the Sheep from the Goats* refers to Matthew XXV, *31-46*; the two groups of animals are a symbol for the human beings of the world on the Day of Judgement, the sheep being on the side of the red angel on the right of Christ, red being symbolic of light and goodness, while the goats on the left of Christ are on the side of the blue angel, signifying darkness and evil.

Plate 29 *Ark of the Covenant.* Apse mosaic. Oratory of Theodulf; Germigny-des-Près, near Orleans, France. First two decades of the 9th century.
This apse mosaic at Germigny-des-Près is the only example left to us of several Carolingian decorative mosaic schemes; it decorated the conch of the apse of the private oratory attached to the sumptuous country residence built for bishop Theodulf, of Orleans (799-818)–an important figure of Charlemagne's court. It depicts two Cherubim guarding the Ark of the Covenant, while two more angels worship before it. It is known that the Frankish clergy under Charlemagne were averse to anthropomorphic representations of God, so that the Ark may perhaps be taken to be a symbol for the presence of the Almighty. The identical pose of the angels could very well mean that they were both drawn from one tracing–a proof of the dependence of Carolingian artists upon Byzantine models; their enormous size in relation to the mosaic area could also imply that the tracing came from

a mosaic of an Annunciation scene in Ravenna or some other centre of Byzantine art.

Plate 30 *Christ Pantocrator.* Monastery at Dafní, Attica, Greece. Late 11th century.
The monastic church at Dafní is dedicated to the *Koimesis*–the Death of the Virgin–and the 'ideal' mosaic system, (see page 20), has therefore been adjusted to accommodate several scenes from the life of the Virgin as told in apocryphal and canonical gospels. However, the bust of the Pantocrator dominates the scheme from the main dome; it is very large, each eye measuring ten inches across. See also figure 7.

Plates 31 and 32 *Virgin and Child* and *The Nativity.* Church of Hosios Loukas, Phocis, Greece. 11th century.
The monastic church at Phocis near Delphi, in Greece, dedicated to St Luke of Stiris, contains the most complete surviving mosaic scheme from the middle Byzantine period (see page 20). St Luke of Stiris lived from the late ninth century until 946; no exact date is known for the foundation of the church dedicated to him or for the mosaics on its vaults and walls, but a period during the second and third quarters of the eleventh century is now accepted and fits the other evidence.

The mosaics of Hosios Loukas are notable for their style of stark austerity which is remarkable even in this period; the style of those at Dafní is much less hieratic and is closer to the flowing, Hellenistic origins of Byzantine art.

The *Virgin and Child* is seen here in the main apse of the church, just above the altar; the *Nativity* is in the north-eastern squinch, below the dome.

Plate 33 *The Emperor Alexander.* North Gallery, Museum of S. Sophia, Istanbul (Constantinople). About 910.
The unusual siting of this single portrait panel, over sixteen

feet above the ground, set into a pier, accounts for the fact that it was only discovered in 1958.

The inscriptions, in the form of cruciform monograms, are inscribed on the four discs on either side of the Emperor. They read: Κύριε βο(ή)θει (τω σω) δού(λ)ω ΑΛΕΞΑΝΔΡΟΣ ὀρθοδόξω πιστῶ δεσπ(ό)τη, and can be translated: 'Lord, help thy servant, the orthodox, faithful Emperor.' From this we know that the portrait represents the Emperor Alexander, who was born in 870-1, the third son of Basil I. After Leo IV's death in May 912, Alexander ruled as sole emperor for 13 months until he died in June 913, and there can be little doubt that this portrait of him dates from that period when he was about 43 years old.

The emperor is shown wearing the full court ceremonial dress, of which the most striking feature is the *loros*, a richly ornamented scarf worn wound round the body; his crown has *perpendulia* of pearls, he holds an orb in his left hand, and in his right the *akakia*–a small pouch filled with dust and wrapped in silk, a symbol of mortality and humility.

Plate 34 *Christ Pantocrator*. Apse mosaic. Monreale Cathedral, Sicily. Late 12th century.
The Cathedral of Monreale was founded and chiefly built in the third quarter of the twelfth century under King William II (1166-1189). Its mosaics are later than the two other chief groups in Sicily, at Cefalù and Palermo, and two historical panels showing the Coronation of William II and the Dedication of the church to the Virgin show that the mosaics were well advanced by the time of the king's death in 1189.

This view of the bust of Christ in the conch of the apse is the culmination and focus of the whole ensemble (see page 21). The Greek inscription, ΙΣ ΧΣ 'Ο ΠΑΝΤΟΚΡΑΤΩΡ means: 'Jesus Christ the Pantocrator' ('the all-powerful'). The text in the open book is in Latin as well as Greek, de-monstrating the eastern and western elements of the decoration; it is from St John VIII, *12*.

Plates 35 and 36 *Christ Enthroned* and *St John the Baptist* Details of the Deesis in the South Gallery, Museum of S. Sophia, Istanbul (Constantinople). Late 13th century.
The figure of St John the Baptist is on the right of that of Christ, the saint bows while the Virgin intercedes on the left. The inscription ΙΣ ΧΣ is the abbreviated Greek form of Jesus Christ, and the title 'Ο ΑΓΙΟΣ 'ΙΩ 'Ο ΠΡΟΔΡΟΜΟΣ means 'Saint John the Forerunner'–the usual Byzantine title for this saint. The style of this mosaic indicates a date in the last quarter of the thirteenth century; with the mosaics of the Kariye Camii, it is one of the most outstanding monuments of the many works carried out in the Capital after the overthrow of Latin rule in 1261.

This sumptuous wall mosaic of the Deesis (Christ enthroned between the Virgin and St John the Baptist) was cleared of its plaster covering in 1933. Although very damaged (of the Virgin, all but the head and right shoulder are missing) it is still perhaps the most impressive mosaic left in Hagia Sophia.

Plates 37 and 38 *The First Seven Steps of the Virgin* and *Theodore Metochites Offering a Model of the Church of St Saviour in Chora to Christ*. The Kariye Camii, Istanbul (Constantinople). About 1310-1320.
The Kariye Mosque near the Edirne Gate in Istanbul was the Church of St Saviour in Chora, meaning 'St Saviour in the fields'; it must therefore have been outside the original Theodosian walls, and so of very ancient foundation. These two scenes are both situated in the inner narthex, the vaults and lunettes of which are chiefly occupied with scenes from the life of the Virgin, taken from the apocryphal gospels. This group of mosaics is dateable to about 1310-1320.

The scene of the *First Seven Steps of the Virgin* is situated on the arch of the vault to the right of this entrance. It illustrates the episode from the Virgin's childhood described in the Protevangelium of St James (VI, *1*): 'And day by day the child waxed strong, and when she was six months old her mother stood her upon the ground to try if she would stand; and she walked seven steps and returned unto her bosom.' Stylistically, this is a very good example of the new pictorial outlook that is shown in Byzantine art in this monument. The figures are shown in movement, and the element of humanity is evident for the first time. Even so, classical motifs such as the figure with billowing veil show direct descent from, for example, the classical Nereid in plate 13.

Theodore Metochites (died 1331), a scholar, scientist and poet, was the Logothete to the imperial treasury when he undertook the enlargement and embellishment of the church. He is depicted here in the traditional form of the donor portrait, wearing court robes and an enormous turban, such as was later adopted by the Turkish conquerors of Constantinople. This mosaic is over the doorway into the main body of the church.

Plate 39 *Entry of Christ into Jerusalem.* St Mark's, Venice. 13th century.
Work was probably begun on the mosaics of St Mark's during the early twelfth century and the first phase continued intermittently through to the late thirteenth or even early fourteenth centuries. They must have been done entirely by Byzantine craftsmen to start with, but an order was made in 1258 that each Greek mosaicist should have two local assistants; as a result of this a local style can be seen to develop, assimilating Byzantine, Romanesque and local Venetian influences.

The *Entry into Jerusalem* is typical of the Veneto-Byzantine mosaic style, with the figures silhouetted against a gold background.

Plate 40 *Death of the Virgin.* (Cavallini). Santa Maria in Trastevere, Rome. About 1291.
Although no inscription now survives, Cavallini's mosaic panels round the apse of the Church of Sta Maria in Trastevere are known to have been signed and are dated to about 1291.

The scene illustrated, the *Death of the Virgin*, has its sources in Byzantine tradition rather than that of Rome; the two groups of mourners, including the Apostles, attend the bier, led by St Paul and St Peter swinging a censer. Christ appears in the centre in a mandorla, holding the Virgin's soul in the form of a child in his veiled hands.

Plate 41 *St Mark in Ecstasy* (Titian). St Mark's, Venice. About 1545.
This mosaic is in the atrium of St Mark's above the principal entrance. Although it is signed by Francesco and Valerio Zuccato, 1545, there is a strong tradition that Titian designed this mosaic for the Zuccato workshop to carry out, and this is confirmed by statements made by Titian in a law-suit against Zuccato in 1563. Also, allowing for the intervention of another hand working in a different medium, the figure style is sufficiently near to Titian's in the 1540s to make his authorship of the design very likely.

Plate 42 *Procession with the Relic of the True Cross* (Gentile Bellini). Detail of the oil painting. Galleria dell'Accademia, Venice. Dated 1496.
Gentile Bellini was one of the official artists of the Venetian Republic, and in this capacity made paintings of some of the main events in the civic and religious life of the city, such as this procession which took place in the large Piazza in

front of St Mark's. Its value to us lies in the great fidelity with which he recorded every detail of the event and its setting, including the decoration on the façade of St Mark's. This detail is the best record that we have of the Byzantine mosaics of the thirteenth or fourteenth centuries that were in the lunette over the second door from the north end of the façade. Of the five original lunette mosaics on the façade all but one have now disappeared, this one being replaced with the scene shown on plate 43.

Plate 43 *The Venetians Venerating the Body of St Mark* (Sebastiano Ricci). Façade of St Mark's, Venice. 1728.
This eighteenth century mosaic serves to demonstrate how the great skill of the later Venetian mosaicists was responsible for the abuse of the medium, destroying its inherent qualities. The result is much nearer to a permanent form of oil-painting than to a true use of mosaic. This lunette mosaic replaced that in the detail on plate 42 when that was destroyed.

Plate 44 *Christ Pantocrator*. Miniature Mosaic Icon. Height 1 ft 9¼ in. × 1 ft 4⅛ in. (54 × 41 cm.). Museo Nazionale del Bargello, Florence. Second half of the 12th century.
This miniature mosaic is clearly a development of the technique and style demonstrated by the icon on plate 45. The *tesserae* have become much smaller, and the modelling more subtle. The severity of the earlier representations remains, but there are suggestions of a softening of the forms that in the next century was to produce such superb works as the Christ in the Deesis in Hagia Sophia (plate 35).

Plate 45 *Christ the Merciful*. Miniature Mosaic. Height 2 ft 5¼ in. × 10¼ in. (74.5 × 52.5 cm.). Ehemals Staatliche Museum, Berlin; Dahlem. About 1100.
This mosaic icon shows the bust of Christ, who is holding a richly decorated Gospel book and is making the act of blessing with the right hand. The inscription IC XC Ο ΕΛΕΗΜΩΝ means 'Jesus Christ the Merciful'. It is an unusual type of representation of Christ.

The very high quality of this work makes its origins in a workshop of Constantinople certain; comparison with the style of representations of the Pantocrator in the mosaics of Dafni, Cefalù and Monreale, suggests a date of about 1100.

Plate 46 *St John Chrysostom*. Miniature Mosaic Icon. 7×5 in. (18 × 13 cm.) Dumbarton Oaks Collection, Washington D.C. Mid fourteenth century.
St John Chrysostom is depicted here in ecclesiastical dress, with a white *omophorion* and a *polystavrion* with red crosses on it; the halo is slightly raised. The saint, who died in 407, is one of the great figures of the early church, and is one of the few saints to receive equal reverence in the Eastern and Western churches. His name 'Ο 'ΑΓΙΟΣ 'ΙΩ(ΑΝΝΗΣ) 'Ο ΧΡΥΣΟΣΤΟΜΟΣ means 'St John the golden-mouthed' and is a reference to his great powers of oratory. His appearance, as described in the texts, was 'fleshless', 'spidery', and 'with high wrinkled forehead and receding hair'; this is rendered in a very life-like manner in this icon.

This mosaic icon is one of the latest of this art form to survive, being produced in Constantinople towards the middle of the fourteenth century, and is known to have come from the monastery of Vatopedi on Mount Athos. The original wood backing can just be seen round the edges.

Plate 47 *Six of the Twelve Major Feasts*. Miniature Mosaic Icon. Size (without frame) 10.6 × 6.2 in. (27 × 16 cm.). Museo dell'Opera del Duomo, Florence. Early 14th century. This portable mosaic panel, set in a silver frame of later date, is one of a pair depicting the twelve major feasts of the Church; those represented here are: The Annunciation;

Nativity; Presentation; Baptism; Transfiguration; and Raising of Lazarus.

The panels were almost certainly made in Constantinople and similarities of style and iconography with the mosaics of the Kariye Camii indicate a date in the early fourteenth century.

Plates 48 and 49 *Sacrificial Knife* and *Mask of Tezcatlipoca*. British Museum, London. 14th century.

These two specimens formed part of a collection of Aztec ritual and ceremonial objects that were given by Montezuma II to Cortes on the Spanish conquest of Mexico in 1519-20. The collection was sent to Spain and presented to the Emperor Charles V. He in turn gave them either to Pope Leo X (died 1521) or to Pope Clement VII when the emperor was crowned King of the Romans by him at Bologna in 1529-30. Both these Popes were members of the Medici family and the Aztec work was absorbed into the Medici private collection, being subsequently dispersed.

The *Sacrificial Knife* has a blade of chalcedony, and the handle, in the form of an eagle warrior, is decorated with mosaic of turquoise, malachite and shell.

The *Mask* is formed from a human skull, onto which turquoise and lignite mosaics have been applied, the eyes being polished iron pyrites.

Both specimens, although presented by an Aztec ruler, are probably Miztec work of the fourteenth century.

Plates 50 and 51 *Mosaic Jewellery*.
Pastoral Landscape. Private Collection, London. Late 18th and early 19th centuries.

Glass *tesserae*, set in a recessed opaque red glass oval. It is now unmounted but was probably originally intended to be mounted in a ring.

Dancing Figure with Flutes. Mosaic Jewellery. Private Collection.

Glass *tesserae* set in a recessed metal oval. Unmounted, but probably intended to be mounted in a ring.

Basket of Flowers. Private Collection. Late 18th and early 19th centuries.

Glass *tesserae* set in a recessed panel of lapis lazuli and mounted in gold for use as a pendant. Some of the smaller flowers and leaves are in 'opus sectile', i.e., cut out to the shape of the object they represent.

Circular Temple. Private Collection. Late 18th and early 19th centuries.

Glass *tesserae* set in opaque black glass or jet. Unmounted, but probably intended as a brooch.

The columns and other straight lines are in 'opus sectile'.

The temple represented may be the Temple of Vesta in the Forum, Rome. The panel was probably made to be a souvenir of Rome.

Full Length Figure in National Costume. Private Collection. Late 18th and early 19th centuries.

Glass *tesserae* set in transparent dark green glass. Unmounted, but probably intended for mounting as a brooch or pendant.

1

2

3

4

6

8

10

12

13

14

16

17

18

19

20

21

23

27

29

ὁ ἅγιος Ἰω̅ ὁ π̅ρόδρομ̅

38

39

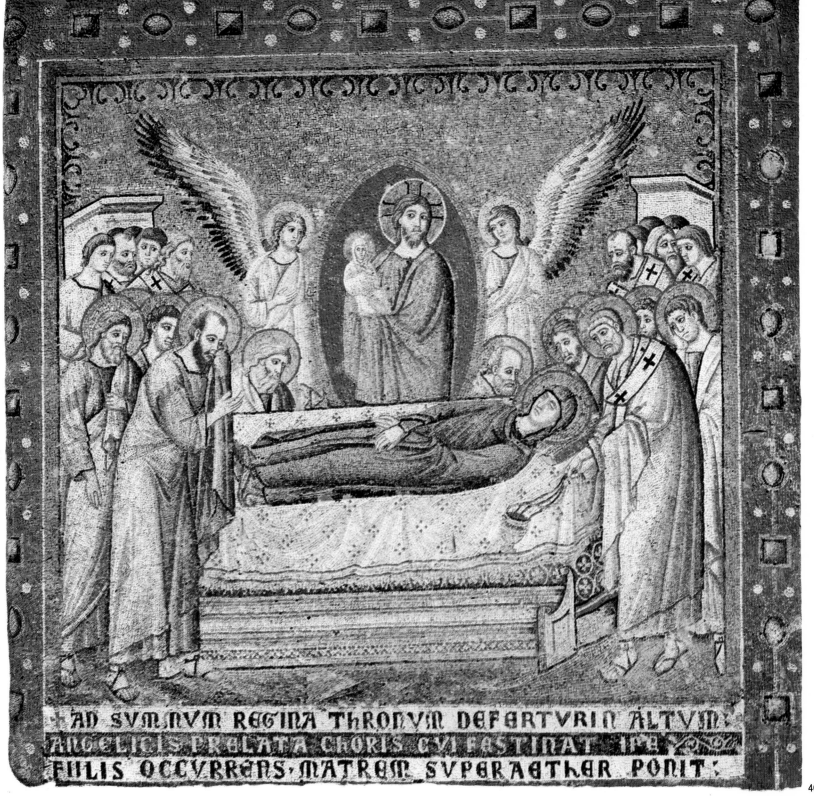

AD SVMNVM REGINA THRONVM DEFERTVRIN ALTVM:
ANGELICIS PROLATA CHORIS CVI FESTINAT IPE
FILIS OCCVRRENS MATREM SVPERAETHER PONIT:

42

43

44

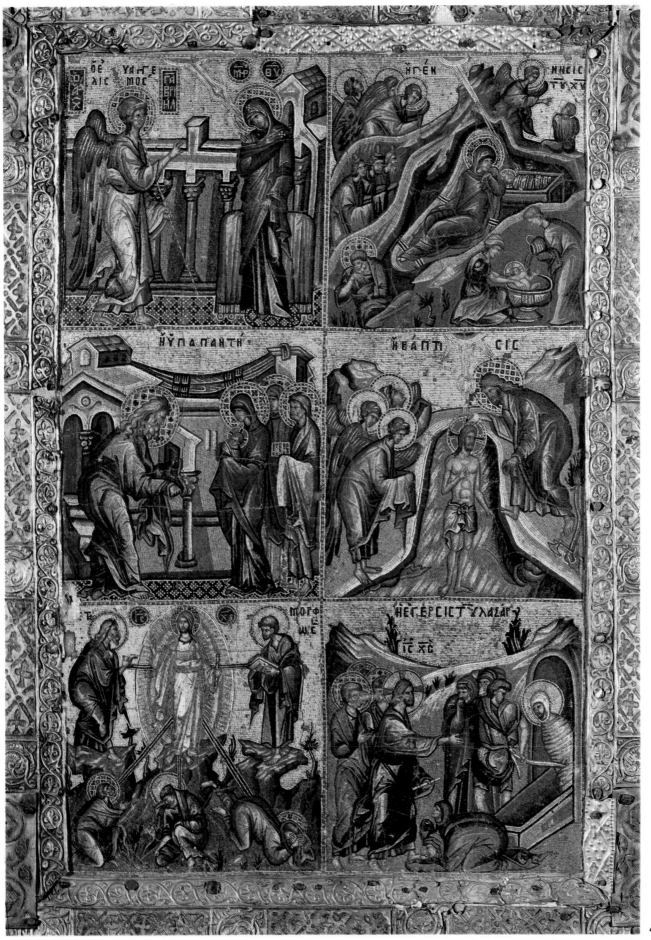

47

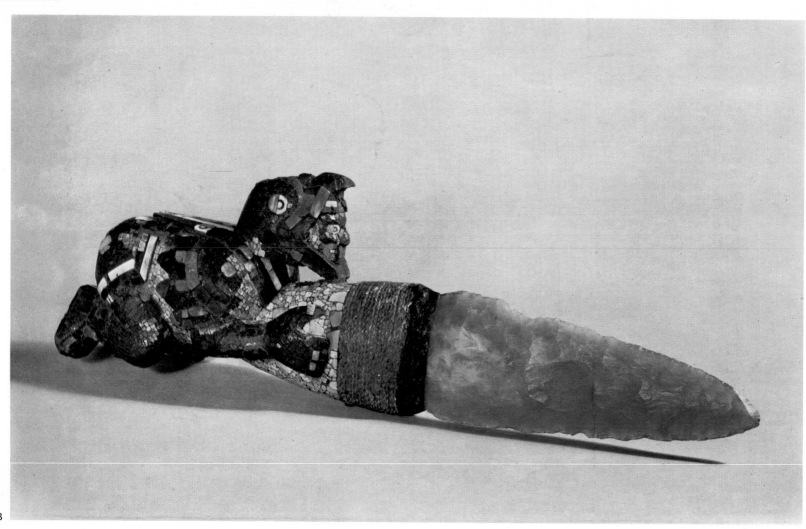

48

50

51